BUCKET LIST BLUEPRINT WORKBOOK

Everything You Need to Start a Bucket List That Brings Your Dreams to Life

-A *Nourish Your Soul* Workbook-

Julie Schooler

Copyright © 2022 Julie Schooler, BoomerMax Ltd

ISBN: 978-0-473-63603-6

All rights reserved. No part of this publication may be reproduced, distributed, or transmitted in any form or by any means, including photocopying, recording, or other electronic or mechanical methods, without the prior written permission of the publisher, except in the case of brief quotations embodied in reviews and certain other non-commercial uses permitted by copyright law.

DISCLAIMER

This workbook is designed to give the reader (that means YOU – the exceptionally awesome person reading this!) some useful tips and ideas about how to create and act upon your personal bucket list.

Bucket list items may pose some risk. The author and publisher advise readers to take full responsibility for their safety and know their limits. What this means for YOU:

- Talk to a health professional before embarking on any increased physical activity.
- Make sure you have full and correct insurance (travel, health, etc.) whenever required.
- Use common sense to keep safe when traveling locally or abroad, and research safety measures that are appropriate in other countries or regions.
- Make sure any equipment you use has been well-maintained.
- Choose reputable companies with the best safety records.
- Tell someone where you are going, what you are doing, and when you expect to be back.
- Choose bucket list items that are within your means financially or for which you are prepared to budget and save.
- Make responsible arrangements so that your work, family and other important areas of life remain in good condition while you pursue your bucket list.

Please, please, please do not choose irresponsible, destructive or illegal items for your bucket list.
The author and publisher accept no responsibility for any harm or loss resulting from your pursuit of the bucket list.
Have fun but keep safe.

*This book is dedicated to my husband, Andrew, who had no idea when we got married that his wife would transform from accountant to adrenaline junkie.
Thank you for tolerating all of my wacky endeavors.*

CONTENTS

Reader Gift: The Happy20   ix

1. Boring To Breathtaking   1
2. What Is A Bucket List And Is It For Me?   7
3. Bucket List Objections   13
4. Why You Absolutely Need A Bucket List   21
5. Seven Unexpected Benefits Of A Bucket List   29
6. Write Your Bucket List   37
7. Bucket List Q&A   53
8. Organize Your Bucket List   61
9. Check Off The First Bucket List Item   69
10. Bucket Lists With Family And Friends   77
11. Supercharge Your Bucket List   85
12. Bucket List Wrap Up   95

Appendix One – My Top40 Bucket List   101
Appendix Two – A Selection of Bucket List Ideas   103
Appendix Three – Bucket List 100 Items Template   109
Reader Gift: The Happy20   117
About the Author   119
Books by Julie Schooler   121
Acknowledgments   123
Please Leave a Review   125
References   127

READER GIFT: THE HAPPY20

There is no doubt that a bucket list will change your life, but it is also important to remember to squeeze the best out every single day. To remind you of this, I created

THE HAPPY20
20 Free Ways to Boost Happiness in 20 Seconds or Less

A PDF gift for you with quick ideas to improve mood and add a little sparkle to your day.

Head to JulieSchooler.com/gift and grab your copy today.

1
BORING TO BREATHTAKING

 'The tragedy of life is not death but what we let die inside of us while we live.' – Norman Cousins

WHAT HAPPENED TO 'CARPE DIEM'?

Each day blends into the next. The same old routine. You have nothing exciting to look forward to. Life seems bland. What is worse is that the days seem to be going by in a blur. Life is rushing by at what seems like an increasing speed each year.

You know there is a bigger life to live. You would love to do something exciting or challenging or meaningful with the good years you have left on this planet. You yearn to get off the rapid and repetitive treadmill of life and actually LIVE. You want to 'carpe diem', seize the day!

But how do you start taking action towards the life of your dreams? What is the first step to planning a life well lived? You need a guide to help you determine what you DO want in life, not what you don't want.

You NEED a bucket list.

SPRING OUT OF BED EACH MORNING

This book will give you practical advice to write the best bucket list personalized for your circumstances, and, most importantly, how to check off items immediately so that you start living the life you always dreamed of.

This entertaining and easy-to-read guide will also cut through the confusion around what a bucket list is and is not, provide compelling reasons why a bucket list is an essential part of life and tell you exactly what to do to discover items for your personal bucket list—even if you have no money, no time and don't want to travel.

In less than a couple of hours this book will give you the exact blueprint to writing your own bucket list. You won't need to spend hours searching for information all over the Internet. You will have a clear direction and won't be confused by conflicting advice. Your new, personalized bucket list will help you spring out of bed every morning with renewed enthusiasm for living, not just existing.

Your life will become breathtaking, not boring.

THE TOP40 BUCKET LIST CHALLENGE

I turned 40 in 2016. This milestone birthday was a catalyst for a big, hairy, audacious goal: check off 40 things from my bucket list in one calendar year. Hence I took on a major challenge—what I called the 'Top40 Bucket List'.

My life is great and I feel extremely blessed with what I have: a lovely suburban home, a kind husband and two loud but gorgeous kids. But a deep desire to do something extra special to mark turning the big 4-0 could not be contained. I wanted to see what it was like to reach my potential, to step out of my comfort zone and to live life even more fully.

I had to work out what bucket list items I wanted to do, then narrow it down to ones that would be possible to do within my time, resources and budget. I read up on how to write bucket lists, got ideas from searching all over the Internet and asked for a lot of help from friends and family.

Surprisingly, I could not find one short, clear, gimmick-free guide on how to write and check off a bucket list, whether over the course of one year or for the rest of my life. I had to scramble around, wasting time trying to work out all these things. A practical blueprint on bucket lists would have made my challenge much easier to manage. I could have started actually doing the things on my bucket list earlier. I also made a lot of mistakes in executing the bucket list and would have done it differently if I had a clear guide.

I distilled the avalanche of information and all my learnings from my Top40 Bucket List challenge into simple and practical tips to help you write your bucket list and then take action to check it off. You gain the best insights and avoid common mistakes around bucket lists. This book contains all the tools, advice and inspiration you need to live a fulfilling and immensely enjoyable life.

Whether you want to do one, ten or a hundred things on a bucket list, and whether you plan to do them in the next week, next year or over the rest of the time you have, this book will help you work out, write out, and most importantly, achieve your heart's desires.

I have written the book that I wanted to read.

BENEFITS OF A BUCKET LIST

Just think how great it will be when you have a written bucket list and you are crossing off items. There are benefits in so many areas.

You will:

- rediscover long-held passions and understand your true self better
- know exactly how to determine what you want in life, not what you don't want
- feel good about yourself for following through on goals
- learn and grow by stepping out of your comfort zone
- wake up each morning with a sense of excitement and zest for life
- spend quality time with friends and family doing fun things together
- lead and inspire others to live life on their terms
- feel like you are living the life you were meant to live, one with excitement, meaning and true joy

THE ONLY BUCKET LIST BOOK YOU WILL EVER NEED

People are happy to recommend this book as it contains everything you need and nothing you don't around bucket lists. They are excited that there is a finally a short book that helps them to easily write and take action on their perfect bucket lists.

Readers are relieved that this book has removed the old association of bucket lists only being for the terminally ill and has made them for anyone. From adrenaline junkies to those more interested in leisurely pursuits, there are tips and ideas that will suit any age, budget and preference.

MY PROMISE TO YOU

This book will make it stress-free and fun to write the bucket list of your dreams. In addition, I promise that you will easily find 100 things for your bucket list that suit your circumstances so perfectly that you will check off at least one item before you even finish reading the book!

It is guaranteed that if you use this book to write a bucket list, you will feel better, family times will be fun again and you will give yourself the best gift of all—a fulfilling life.

Your Ideal Life is Waiting

Do not leave it another dreary and mundane day to read this book. Be the happy, energized and accomplished person you always thought you would be—not when you are too old or ill to do anything, but right now. Read this book today and take action on your ideal life.

Read this Before You Kick the Bucket

Step off the dull treadmill of day-to-day life and turn your dreams into memories. Don't wait until you almost 'kick the bucket' to read this book! Bucket lists are for the living, not the nearly dead. Start now, before you are too sick and frail to enjoy anything.

This book will reignite that spark you once had. You will learn how to focus on what you really want—to live a life by design, not by default. Ultimately, this bucket list book will lead you to be more enriched, fulfilled and happy, every single day, for the rest of your life.

Workbook Note

In each chapter of this workbook there will be questions and prompts so that you can write down your answers and ideas that are designed to help you in the process of bucket list creation. Feel free to write as much or as little as you like. You can even skip sections. But please, no matter what, jot down at least a few ideas for your own bucket list (Chapter 6).

2
WHAT IS A BUCKET LIST AND IS IT FOR ME?

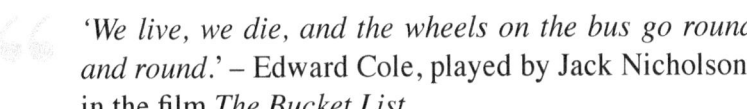 *'We live, we die, and the wheels on the bus go round and round.'* – Edward Cole, played by Jack Nicholson, in the film *The Bucket List*

WHAT IS A BUCKET LIST?

A bucket list is a record of the most important things you want to do, dreams you want to fulfill, special items you want to have or own, people you want to meet, and experiences, accomplishments and challenges you want to overcome in your lifetime.

In short, a bucket list is a list of things you want to do before you die. Actually, let's add one word into the shorter definition.

> A bucket list is a WRITTEN list of things you want to do before you die

The writing down part is an essential element of a bucket list. More on writing and its importance later.

The 'bucket' part comes from the expression 'kick the bucket', which is a euphemism for dying, although no one quite knows why that association was made. A bucket list, therefore, is closely linked with a terminal diagnosis or being old and sick. The term was popularized in the 2007 film *The Bucket List* starring Jack Nicholson and Morgan Freeman.

Removing this association with imminent mortality is one of the main objectives of this book. Sure, we are all going to die, but a bucket list can—and should—be written by anyone, especially those of us who are fortunate enough to be alive and well.

A hot air balloon ride is a 'classic' bucket list item. One hot air balloon operator admitted that he gives half-price rides to terminal cancer patients as he gets so many enquiries from them. That is one of the saddest things I have ever heard. Please, please book your hot air balloon trip when you are not sick, even if it does cost you full price. Believe me, it is worth every penny.

We are all going to die one day, so you can't ignore your own mortality, but creating a bucket list need not be linked so tightly to it. Hopefully picking up this book will inspire you to start yours today, not when you are nearly dead.

> Having a bucket list isn't about dying.
> It is about living.

Who is this Book For and Not For?

I don't want to waste your time, so I will be as straight up as possible about whom this book is for and not for and how you should read it.

This book is for anyone from 9 to 90 who wants to live a more fulfilling and fun life. As noted above, it is not just for the terminally ill or nearly dead. That is an out-of-date association. The new bucket list definition is a rejuvenated and inclusive one for everyone.

Bucket lists are NOT for you if you just want to follow the same old routine day in and day out. They are NOT for you if you only want to do what society expects of you. And they are certainly NOT for you if you simply want to work hard and delay your enjoyment of life until you are old and retired.

This book and bucket lists in general ARE for you if you want a challenge, desire some adventure and need some variety in your life. Chapter Four discusses the deep human need for variety in depth. A bucket list is for anyone who is still curious about life and who has a mindset of wanting to experiment. This sense of just trying things out means that sometimes you will fail at things and sometimes things don't happen as you would like, and you will learn to deal with that.

Most importantly, this book will help you create a bucket list so you don't get to the end of your life with regrets. The main regrets of the dying will be touched on later, but for now, let's keep it light and say that bucket lists are for people who want to create great memories.

Be the person at the office with the interesting weekend story of riding on a tandem bike or learning to surf. Enjoy planning that trip to the Tuscan cooking school you have always dreamed about. And look forward to recounting that time you became a clown for a day or were an extra in a movie to your grandchildren.

THE TOP40 BUCKET LIST

One morning, not long after I turned 39, I woke up with a ridiculous idea. I am turning 40. There are at least 40 things on my bucket list. I could attempt to check off 40 bucket list items in a year. Some of those may not be possible, but I could get more ideas. I quickly started scouring the Internet for inspiration and asking friends for suggestions.

I knew deep in my bones that this was what I wanted to do in order to embrace this birthday milestone. I was excited. My 'Top40

Bucket List' was born. Some items were cheap, local, and even dull. 'Grow sunflowers' was one item that would seem modest to others. Some I had to plan and budget for—traveling to another city to see 'The World of Wearable Arts' was one of the more expensive and time consuming items. I definitely had to consider finances, family commitments and other constraints, but I had a list of 40 bucket list items I was intent on checking off.

What a way to celebrate turning 40!

You probably have two immediate questions—what were these 40 items and did I succeed in doing them all? The Top40 Bucket List is listed in Appendix One, but don't peek just yet. I said don't peek! You will be writing your own bucket list soon, and it is better not to have too many ideas from someone else inside your brain when you do. Look at my list after you take a stab at the first draft of your bucket list.

For now, know that—spoiler alert—YES! I succeeded in checking off every single one of the 40 bucket list items during 2016. I ended on a literal high note when on the 30th of December 2016, I jumped out of a plane in a tandem skydive.

Why I Wrote This Book

It was a LOT of hard work figuring out the exact 40 items to do, writing them down, scheduling them in and working out how to take action on them. I had to adjust around travel, budget and family constraints, keep motivated all year long and overcome a lot of fear (tandem skydives are not for the faint hearted!).

What made it harder was that I had absolutely no frame of reference. You will still have to figure out your own bucket list and face your fears; no one can do that for you. But now that you have this book in your hands, coming up with your own personal bucket list—and of course, starting it and checking it off—will be much easier for you.

I wrote this book so that the next person who wants to prioritize a bit of fun or embrace some new challenges can write their perfect bucket list. They don't have to do something crazy like cross off 40 items in a year, but knowing they are moving towards even one long held wish is exciting.

This book is here to help you focus on what you really want. You will feel a major sense of achievement in marking off items. And you will grow as a person as you step out of your comfort zone and complete a challenge that was only a dream.

If you are a 'get to the point' person, then feel free to skip the next three chapters and go straight to Chapter Six. That plus Chapters Seven, Eight and Nine are the main ones you will need to create your own best bucket list and start taking action on it. However, if you still need a bit more convincing about why a bucket list is not only a good idea, but essential to a life well lived, keep reading right through.

This is a short book but—and this is not said lightly—it will change your life.

WHY ARE YOU READING THIS BOOK?

What attracted you to this book? Would you like to understand exactly what a bucket list is? Do you want to create a bucket list from scratch or revise one you already have started? Perhaps you need more ideas? Write down why you are here. Know that no matter what, you are in the right place.

_____

_____

_____

_____

JULIE SCHOOLER

3

BUCKET LIST OBJECTIONS

 'Life isn't about finding yourself. Life is about creating yourself.' – George Bernard Shaw

BUT BUT BUT

You are aged between 9 and 90, you want some more fun and adventure, and you kind of like the idea of a little book that will change your life. BUUUUUUTTTTT, you still have some objections to this whole bucket list malarkey. Boy, you are a hard nut to crack! Let's address these objections up front now so we can keep moving to the good bits, shall we?

'IT FEELS LIKE ANOTHER TO-DO LIST AND I HAVE ONE OF THOSE already (that I don't do)'

Contrary to the fact that it has 'list' in its name, a bucket list is NOT a to-do list. Think of it more as a 'capture list' or a 'priority list'. It is where you write down your most important dreams and goals to make you feel happier and more fulfilled. You are pinpointing what you really want in life and in a way excluding (for now at least) what you don't want.

We live in a time in which we have the technology, transport and resources to help us go anywhere and do anything, but no one can 'do it all'. Your bucket list will tap into your deepest desires and help you focus on the best things in life for you. It will only become a TO-DO when you schedule it in your diary or calendar.

'IT SOUNDS GREAT, BUT DON'T HAVE TIME RIGHT NOW FOR A bucket list'

Oh yes, the time excuse. The old cliché of 'work' and 'family' taking priority. Let's counter these jaded responses with some equally tired but oh so incredibly true sayings. You only live once. Life is not a dress rehearsal. Let me remind you that if you are happier, then others around you will be, too, and you will be better at what you do.

Look, we all have the same 24 hours in a day, and someone out there is swimming with whales and you are not. You are busy being busy without adding value into your life.

> Our culture celebrates busyness!
> Don't confuse this with living a fulfilling life.

How many times have you checked Facebook or Twitter already today? What if in those few seconds, you looked up flights to Paris, or how many days at Disney World are recommended, or how much a Caribbean cruise would cost?

You can spend a lot of time focusing on other people in social media, but wouldn't it feel a lot better if you directed your attention onto little tasks to put in place a dream trip? You may not have time for travel now, but you do have spare moments in the day in which you can plan your next vacation.

To actually complete bucket list items, you could do things on your bucket list as a family. Take the kids rock climbing or learn origami together. Or you can stack bucket list items together. This will be discussed in a later chapter, but for example, when I wrote down that I wanted to see the 'The World of Wearable Arts' in Wellington, I found a couple of other things to do in Wellington and added them to my bucket list.

Overall, delegate or eliminate things in your life that are not top priority. Say "no" in the nicest possible way. Push your bucket list to the front, or you will end up doing it when you are nearly dead, or not at all.

'I CAN'T THINK OF THINGS FOR MY BUCKET LIST'

Don't worry, you have come to the right place. There are plenty of questions and exercises in here to prompt your imagination. In addition, there are ways to think about your bucket list in terms of categories that will help get the brainstorming going.

There is also a little-known thing called the 'Internet' and that does have a lot of ideas as well. Your imagination may need a little nudge as it has been swamped by boring daily routines and you have forgotten how to be child-like and playful. At the moment, don't worry about having no ideas. By the end of this book you will have plenty.

'I WANT TO DO EVERYTHING'

You may think you want to do everything. The Internet may be to blame here as you can see everything is possible. Visit every country in the world. Taste all the different foods. As Julie Andrews sings: 'Climb Every Mountain'. Again, I would contend this is due to your creativity being stifled. You want everything because that is easier than thinking in specifics about what you really want.

If it helps, start writing a 'NOT bucket list'. People often find it easier to know what they don't want to do. I knew there was no way I would be ever be coaxed into doing a bungy jump. No way. Never. What are your never evers? Strangely, this will help filter down to more specific bucket list ideas that you actually do want to do.

'I don't have the money for a bucket list'

First, remember this is a capture list; you are not scheduling anything just yet. And second, there are hundreds of ideas you can do for very little or no money. Over half of the ideas on my Top40 Bucket List cost under $200. Many were free. Only one cost over $1,000.

With regard to travel, you can use air points or reward points and look for good deals. Remember also that budgeting becomes easier and more fun with a specific travel goal in mind. Or you can use your bucket list items to save you money—a two-for-one deal. Creating a special signature dish with your own secret recipe will save you the cost of takeaways or eating out. Teaching yourself the ukulele or mastering a card trick are simple and low-cost ideas to do at home. Deciding to run a marathon will keep you fit without the expensive gym fees. Think outside the box.

'Isn't a bucket list a 'nice to have' rather than an essential part of life?'

Another way of saying this objection is, "What is the point of a bucket list? It seems kind of frivolous."

A bucket list is as far from silly or shallow as you can get. In fact, it is not really about doing all those external things at all. A bucket list taps into your deepest wants and desires. It allows you to get out of your comfort zone and therefore grow as a person. And it gives you a sense of discipline in planning, plus a feeling of accomplishment in achieving items on the list.

You don't just take away memories, but a surer sense of self, and that is priceless.

'SHOULDN'T I FOCUS ON THE JOURNEY, NOT THE DESTINATION?'

In our busy-centric world we focus on neither the journey nor the destination! At least having a bucket list puts an end goal in sight. It is well documented that successful people begin with the end in mind, so maybe the classic 'journey' argument is not that important.

Luckily with bucket lists, as well as a goal, there is a lot of journey involved. You can use spare moments to plan larger bucket list items and your anticipation of an upcoming event is an invaluable source of happiness. (More about this later.) Don't use whether the journey or destination is better as an excuse not to have a bucket list at all.

'I DON'T WANT EVERYTHING I DO PLANNED OUT. WHERE IS THE spontaneity?'

Some objectors will say that making a clear list allows no room for spontaneity in life. Having a list of set goals takes all the fun out of it. But without any goals there is no fun to start with!

You can still be spontaneous, but at least with a bucket list already prepared, you will have an inkling of the type of activities and experiences you want to do. If something comes up that is not on the list but speaks to you, then write it down and do it as well. If you are at the beach for surf lessons and notice that there are jet skis for hire, then go for it! You can change your bucket list at any time.

'ISN'T HAVING A BUCKET LIST KIND OF SELFISH?'

Having a bucket list is a way of taking action to increase your happiness, connect with others and grow as a person through undertaking challenges. It is one of the least selfish things you can ever do!

Creating a bucket list enables you to rediscover long held dreams and find out more about your authentic self. It also shows you as an action taker, a person who puts themselves out there and is prepared to fail. In other words, it shows that you are a leader, and goodness knows, we need more positive role models in leadership.

Yes, at times when I was arranging yet another weekend around a Top40 Bucket List item, I felt a bit self-centered. But without the list driving me, my family and I wouldn't have had a picnic on that little-known island close by, my husband and I would have had a sedate date night instead of riding on a tandem bike together, and I certainly wouldn't have spent money at businesses in other cities. Doing the Top40 Bucket List made me a better person, and I also got to spend quality time with friends and family. Where is the selfish part in that?

If that still doesn't convince you, then link some of your bucket list items to charitable endeavors such as doing a fun run that sponsors a charity. Or put down 'work in a soup kitchen for a day', 'give blood' or 'learn CPR' as things you would like to do.

'ISN'T A BUCKET LIST RISKY?'

A bucket list does have a risk element to it. There is no denying that. But it has about the same amount of risk as life itself. None of us gets out of here alive! You need to balance wanting to live life as fully as possible with your tolerance for risk.

There is a disclaimer at the start of this book and it will be recapped here. Talk to a health professional before embarking on any change in physical activity. Make sure you have full and correct insurance. Use common sense to keep safe while traveling. Choose reputable companies with the best safety records. Please do not put highly dangerous, irresponsible or illegal items on your list. The ideas in this book are only suggestions. Ultimately, the choices you make for your bucket list are entirely your responsibility.

What You Are Really Saying

Most of the questions and statements above, especially the last one, are your mind's attempts to procrastinate and tell you a bucket list is 'too hard' because there is fear involved.

These objections are a way of saying you are scared. And that is natural. Of course you are scared. Scared of failing. Scared of stepping out of your comfort zone. Scared of doing things that are not 'normal' in our society. A bit of fear is healthy and won't miraculously disappear. More on fear in the next chapter, but for now understand that the only way to eliminate fear is to do the thing you fear.

We have covered many, if not all, of your objections, but we are not done with the dark parts yet. The next chapter explains why most people will never write a bucket list even though they absolutely need one.

WHAT ARE YOUR OBJECTIONS TO MAKING A BUCKET LIST?

Write down the objections from above that resonate most with you and add in any further objections you may have.

_____

_____

_____

_____

WHAT IS THE UNDERLYING REASON FOR YOUR OBJECTIONS?

Do you agree that fear is the main underlying reason? If so, fear of what exactly? If not, what is it instead?

4
WHY YOU ABSOLUTELY NEED A BUCKET LIST

 'In the end what matters is how much happiness they have brought to those they love and how much time they spent doing things they themselves loved.' – Bronnie Ware

NEGATIVE THINKING

What has stopped you from living the life of your dreams?

The reason you are not doing what you want in life is because of your thoughts. Your thoughts are just thoughts. They are not real things but only whispers and conversations inside your mind. Most people's thoughts are about 80% negative.

Most people think about what they don't want.

So if your mind is shaping your future, but all you are thinking about is what you don't want, then the world around you gives you exactly that. So you get less fun and challenge in your life because you don't want to feel scared. You get less time for your hobbies and passions because you don't want to look out of place or not serious enough. You get less opportunity to explore, as you don't want to leave your comfort zone.

You don't live the life of your dreams because your silly, little, negative, untruthful thoughts tell you that they are impossible and no one lives like that.

Let's get this straight right now: you are responsible for your life; you create your life. Not the latest political scandal, not climate change, not a nuclear or terrorism threat. You.

If you are just going through the motions in life controlled by fear, then it is up to you to find a way to change that. Hint: picking up this book is a very good start.

You may be kicking yourself right about now, but know that everyone is like this until they wake up.

It ends today! Don't let the story you tell yourself stop you from being truly happy and fulfilled.

The Comfort Zone

For example, people think they don't want to leave their comfort zones, as they feel nice and familiar, and they feel safe and in control of their environments. Going to work, coming back to your home, watching TV, these are all nice at times. Being in your comfort zone is comfortable, but after a while it actually starts to hurt you. You start to feel unenthused and jaded with your routine existence.

Stepping out of your comfort zone and trying new things leads to growth, and growth is necessary for a fulfilling life. More about this below but hopefully this gives you a little taste of what changing one negative thought can do to improve your life.

The real magic happens outside of the comfort zone. So if the magic happens there, why do you want to stay inside your comfort zone?

It is because of your NEED for certainty.

THE SIX HUMAN NEEDS

Author, coach and personal development expert, Tony Robbins, has popularized the theory that we all have six human needs. These are needs, not wants. We crave these on a deep level.

We have a need for **certainty**—to feel safe and secure and to know that our expectations will be met. In apparent opposition to this, we have a need for **variety**—to have surprises and excitement in our lives (taking a vacation, for example). We also have a need for **significance**—to feel important and that our lives have meaning. On the other side of the coin, we have a need for **love and connection**. We can't be too individual, too significant, or we often lose connection with others.

These four needs are our core or personality needs. The other two needs are for **growth** and **contribution**. These are our secondary or spiritual needs, and not everyone gets these two needs met as the other four can take priority. This is an extremely concise description, and I encourage every one of you to look up Tony Robbins's explanation of these needs in more detail.

Many people intuitively sense a truth in 'The Six Human Needs'. But you don't even have to believe it. They run your life regardless of whether you think they do or not. How you try and meet these needs—in positive, negative or neutral ways—plus which needs you emphasize, have a major impact on your life.

WHAT IS YOUR CURRENT TOP HUMAN NEED? BE HONEST!

Choose from certainty, variety, significance, connection, growth and contribution. Think about what drives you and how your interact with the world. There are no wrong answers.

_____

_____

_____

WHAT WOULD YOU LIKE YOUR TOP HUMAN NEED TO BE?

Choose from certainty, variety, significance, connection, growth and contribution. Think about how you would like to show up in the world.

_____

_____

_____

The Needs for Certainty and Variety

The need that pervades life the most is the need for certainty. People innately want to feel safe, secure, and yes, comfortable. You desire control, order and predictability because you think your life depends on it. And, as demonstrated with the insight into comfort zones above, this is helpful, to a degree, but it can also be harmful.

Your need for certainty helps you find stable work, a place to live, and it builds your family and community around you, but it also allows you to fall into the same routine and you get bored. You get bored because you have another equally important need; the need for variety, but it often gets ignored or minimized, as certainty is so tremendously important to you.

The need for variety is why you have vacation time. It is the reason workweeks have weekends attached. It is why people make time for hobbies. You need to prioritize it just as much as certainty or you stay the same and don't grow, and then life becomes a monotonous, dull effort. Think how great you feel after you spend a weekend away. Only a couple of days and you have a renewed energy and zest for life.

> One of the best things about a bucket list is that it meets your deep needs for certainty and variety at the same time.

Certainty: You get to organize your thoughts, plan things you want to cross off and have a system for doing things you always wanted to do.

Variety: you get to do new things, expand your world and challenge yourself. You thought a bucket list was an extra, a 'nice to have' thing in your life and now you realize it is absolutely essential for meeting two of your primary needs.

So why do people let the need for certainty override their equally important need for variety? Why do people not like change? Because of their deeply ingrained fears.

FEAR AND DEATH

Some people are better at dealing with fears than others, but we ALL have fear. We fear different things, but ultimately, as Susan Jeffers points out in her classic self-help book *Feel the Fear and Do It Anyway*, we have an underlying fear of 'I can't handle it'. We fear that we can't handle whatever life brings us.

This makes sense in relation to our fear of death. We fear death because although it is inevitable, we are not sure when it will happen, whether it will be painful and how our loved ones will cope without us. It is very important, therefore, to stop and discuss death for a little bit, as checking off a bucket list is—for better or worse—intrinsically linked to death, or its euphemism, 'kicking the bucket'.

Because we fear death, we shut out the very prospect of it. We need to stop pretending that we will live forever, that we have all the time in the world, and face our own mortality straight on. Although I don't like bucket lists to be associated with terminal diagnoses, perhaps remembering that in one way or another, we are all 'terminal' will help us live life more fully.

Time is limited, whether we deny that fact or not.

In the end, we all need to face up to our very real mortality. Let us dance with our fear of death. That will move our energies from a material life of comfort controlled by fear to a life of purpose, fulfillment and fun. Start with accepting the limited days you have left and then think about what you really want out of life.

The alternative to designing a fulfilling life is coming to the end of your life with regrets. People can regret a whole range of things, but, as noted in Bronnie Ware's book, *The Top Five Regrets of the Dying*, many people wish they had lived a life that was more true to who they were, let themselves be happier and not worked so hard. Starting your own bucket list will go a long way towards eliminating these regrets from your own deathbed.

Do you want to keep on having the same life you have had so far, securely ensconced in your tiny comfort zone, prioritizing your need for certainty and controlled by your fears so much that you die with regrets? Or do you want to live life on your terms, working out and then taking action on what your heart desires?

This will be said a few times in this book, but you have choices. You can choose to live in fear and not do the things you want to do most in life then die with regrets, OR you can choose to face your fears, dance with them and ultimately eliminate them by doing what you love. Both choices are hard. <u>Choose your hard</u>.

If all this talk of stepping out of your comfort zone, embracing your need for variety and facing your fear of dying doesn't persuade you to create your bucket list straight away, then the next chapter will seal the deal with seven unexpected benefits of having a bucket list.

ADDITIONAL NOTES

This is HEAVY stuff! Write down anything else that has come up for you after reading this chapter.

_____

_____

_____

_____

_____

_____

_____

_____

_____

_____

5
SEVEN UNEXPECTED BENEFITS OF A BUCKET LIST

 'It is not the years in your life but the life in your years that counts.' - Adlai E. Stevenson

THE SUPER SEVEN

Here are seven, perhaps slightly unexpected, benefits of a bucket list:

1. A BUCKET LIST BUILDS INTEGRITY

In order to create a bucket list, you must work first at brainstorming about what you want. As noted earlier, this is hard as most people are thinking about what they don't want. Then you need to prioritize what you are able to do and when you will do it. As you have access to everything in life, the ability to focus and prioritize is now a rare and highly sought after skill. Then you actually have to execute your plan, which is perhaps the most difficult step of all.

All these stages to a bucket list create diligence and conscientiousness and ultimately show integrity—in that you do what you say you are going to do. It shows you plan, take action and follow through to the end. Integrity is an extraordinary trait these days. Other people—friends, work colleagues and especially your kids—appreciate and are inspired by it, and you get to feel great about yourself as well.

Doing my Top40 Bucket List was a mighty challenge, stressful and hard work at times, but even now I still feel proud and extremely satisfied that I crossed it all off.

2. A Bucket List Allows You to Fail

You may be worried about creating a bucket list and then never marking it all off. Or that you haven't chosen the 'right' things. Or that you will attempt to do them and they won't work. Or you will give up.

Let me tell you now, you WILL fail with your bucket list!

You probably will never check it all off, and things won't happen the way you want them to some of the time. The thing about a bucket list is all of that doesn't matter. Actually a bucket list allows you to fail in an area of your life in which the consequences of failing aren't really that high.

I crossed off all my Top40 Bucket List items, but I also 'failed' on three of them. I said I would 'catch a fish' when in the end I went fishing but didn't catch anything. Note: wording of your bucket list items is important! Two other items were not done as I envisaged, either, but the point is that I attempted them.

Failure is a part of life. The only people who don't fail are the ones who don't try. Your true character is built not on whether you fail but on how and when you pick yourself back up again. Maybe next time you will fail better! Do you know how many people care that I 'failed' at those three things? Zero. No one cares. Overall, people are impressed that I made an effort to do 40 bucket list items in one year. No one really cares about the details. Please look at failing as a good thing.

3. A BUCKET LIST MAKES YOU FEARLESS

Actually doing things on your bucket list does not automatically make you fearless. But as I mentioned earlier, the only way to beat fear is to move through it. Do the very thing that frightens you so that you are no longer scared of it. Know that the anticipation of the actual thing is far scarier than the thing is, so if you schedule it and do it, you reduce a lot of inner angst and conflict.

Stepping out of your comfort zone by doing things on a bucket list makes doing more things you find fearful—either on or off the bucket list—easier to do. Fear diminishes, and confidence and self-esteem improve, the more steps you take outside your comfort zone. This leads to personal growth, which is a key component to lifelong happiness, as will be explained in detail in a later chapter.

A surprising addition to the fearless benefit is that doing some of the things on my bucket list that terrified me the most (especially the tandem skydive) made other things seem less frightening. Since finishing the Top40 Bucket List I have seen a film, *The Cabin in the Woods* that I previously decided was too terrifying to watch. It was fine. I am looking forward to where my newfound courage takes me. I may one day be quite fine being in close quarters with a spider.

4. A BUCKET LIST GIVES YOU CONTROL

This has been talked about in the previous chapter, but almost ironically, having a big list of things to do that are outside your comfort zone brings you a much-needed sense of control in life. You have certainty about variety and are therefore meeting two of your core needs in one go. This is very powerful.

A bucket list gives control via a few mechanisms: it brings about a sense of purpose in life, something to strive for, to accomplish. It gives your current work more meaning as it is not just paying the bills but helping you budget for the life you dreamed of. And a bucket list helps start or stop habits without using willpower. You decide to run a marathon, so you get in the habit of getting your running shoes on and going. You decide to snorkel at the Great Barrier Reef, so you start eating better to fit back into your swimsuit. You decide to take the family on that Disney Cruise next year, so you put aside some savings each week for it. That bigger goal makes the habit changes easier to bear.

The rest of the world may be going to hell in a hand basket, but this one thing, your personal bucket list, is a way of controlling exactly how you want to live before the zombie apocalypse actually happens.

5. A Bucket List Is Inspirational

The fact you are motivating yourself and directing energy to fun and challenging goals strikes a chord with many people. Your friends, family and especially your children will see that dreaming big is not only allowed but is also accessible with plans and goals.

> Having a bucket list lets you become a better version of YOU.

Once you start checking items off, you not only get to feel successful and accomplished but others around you unwittingly learn valuable life lessons about failure, success and determination, among other things.

In a way, a bucket list could be considered an inspirational gift. You thought you were scribbling down a little list, but instead you were creating a magnificent legacy for now and for generations to come.

6. A BUCKET LIST SHOWS FUN IS ESSENTIAL

Let's face it, in today's world where we all worship at the altar of busyness and distractedness, when is the last time you have had good clean fun? I don't mean finding happiness at the bottom of that glass of pinot or in the latest scroll or swipe, but in real life: backyard waterslide kind of fun. You need fun like you need work and family. You have just forgotten how essential it is.

If you have kids, embracing fun is even more critical. A bucket list will help you rediscover your carefree, playful and daring side. Aren't these attributes you would want your kids to see in you plus have in droves themselves? At the very least, a bucket list is a good way to stop boredom in its tracks. There are plenty of ideas for bucket list items to do as a family in Chapter Ten.

And if spending time with loved ones, being active and discovering new things aren't enough benefits, perhaps think of fun items on a bucket list another way. Many of us crave something sweet and think we will find it in the back of the pantry or fridge. But this craving for something sweet is not a nutritional need, it is a deep need for more light and laughter in your life. So do something nice for yourself that doesn't involve chocolate: create a bucket list and give yourself the chance to have some sweet and essential fun.

7. A BUCKET LIST FILLS YOUR CUP

Life today is filled with 'shoulds'. You should help others and should think about the environment and should live mindfully in your community. But this is very hard when you don't feel like you have much to give. You are often exhausted and overwhelmed with your life. You need your cup to be filled up before you can be generous without feeling resentful about it.

A bucket list is a perfect project to fill your cup. Doing something that fills you up inside and gives you a boost of joy spreads happiness to your loved ones and the world at large. You meet new people, appreciate other cultures and spend quality time with your kids. Positive emotions are useful and essential as they are linked to better health, longevity, productivity and social wellness.

As speaker and author, Lisa Nichols, eloquently describes it, fill your cup up so that it is overflowing onto the saucer and only then "serve" from your saucer.

Build a bucket list and create a win-win with the world.

OTHER BENEFITS OF A BUCKET LIST

Of course, a bucket list has a lot of other benefits not listed here in the areas of health, relationships and finances. It gets you off the sofa and outside in the fresh air that your grandmother always said was good for you. It provides the perfect reason to spend screen-free time with loved ones. It helps you to budget for the most important things you want to do with your hard-earned cash.

All the benefits of a bucket list, but especially the seven unexpected benefits above, hopefully get you amped up for writing your list. Because the next chapter is where the work begins. You WILL have 100 items on your bucket list by the end of Chapter Six.

WHAT ARE YOUR TOP BENEFITS OF A BUCKET LIST?

Write down the benefits from above that resonate most with you and add in any further benefits.

_____

_____

_____

_____

Bucket List Blueprint WORKBOOK

6

WRITE YOUR BUCKET LIST

 'One day your life will flash before your eyes. Make sure it's worth watching.' – Gerard Way

YOU ARE READY!

The time has come to take action. By the end of this chapter you will have 100 items written down on the first draft of your bucket list. You may have come along for the motivational ride in the first few chapters, or you may be the 'show me the money' type of person who skipped straight here. Wherever you came from, if you have landed on this chapter YOU ARE READY.

Let's do this!

Yes, I said 100 bucket list items. Written down. Don't run away. This will be broken down into two easy steps. First a massive brainstorm of ideas and then a second stage that uses questions and prompts.

The most important thing to remember during this two-part exercise is to not only capture everything but also to really focus on and prioritize things YOU want to see, do, be and have. Once you start, you will find the ideas pour forth, so don't try and contain that fountain, but keep going back inside yourself and notice whether this is something YOU really want.

Yet Another Benefit

One benefit not explicitly touched on in the previous chapter is that a bucket list helps you zero in on your true desires, focus in on what you really, really, really want in life and remind yourself of your long-held dreams. In other words, you tap into your own passions and end up knowing more about yourself. Getting a deeper understanding of the most important person in your life (you) is crucial to living a more fulfilling life.

We live in an age in which anything is possible and doable. You can book a trip into space if you want. But all the way through the exercises in this chapter, ask yourself if this is a 'HELL YEAH' bucket list item. As author and entrepreneur, Derek Sivers, states, "If you're not saying 'HELL YEAH!' about something, say 'no'".

Do you really want to bungy jump, or are you putting it down because it is a typical bucket list item? By all means, don't mute yourself at this point, get it down and you can remove it later. But capturing what you really want is a core part of this exercise.

This is meant to help you prioritize, streamline and get clear on your bucket list choices, not to overwhelm you. It may feel overwhelming at first, but in the end you will feel clearer about what you want. You will end up more in tune with yourself than you have ever been before.

Writing a bucket list is all about getting in touch with your truest, innermost desires, and creating massive personal intention to achieve them. You are only doing the first part here—tapping into you. Take the action part right out of the equation for now. Do not think about how you will actually check off the items.

STEP ONE: GET IT DOWN!

A key component to a bucket list is that it is written down. Writing it down makes it real, gets your thoughts in order and is a permanent record of your wants and dreams. You are more likely to achieve what you have written down. Do not skip this step. The writing part is very powerful.

Get it down!

What you need: something on which to write out your bucket list— a blank Word or other text document on your computer, or a large piece of paper or the back of an envelope. You are welcome to use the basic template in Appendix Three at the back of this book. Anything will do. Gather up some pens or colored markers as well, if needed. Then find something with which to time yourself for up to thirty minutes—a watch, phone timer or a giant hourglass, for example.

Don't do anything else in the time you set aside for this exercise. Don't check spellings of place names or what the capital city of a country is or if there is a surf school nearby. And for goodness sake, don't check the Internet for ideas, not at this point. You have a brain, so use it.

Now brainstorm, free write or mind map EVERYTHING you have always wanted to do, see, have, be, meet, etc. You KNOW in your heart what you want.

Have fun with this creative exercise. Be silly, invoke your curiosity, think outside the box. Think about fun things, challenging things, short-term activities, long-term pastimes, local places to visit and trips abroad. Think of your interests, hobbies, and passions. Dream big. Anything goes.

Get it down!

Write in short bullet points or long, descriptive paragraphs. Know that anything can be changed or deleted later. Don't worry if it seems more like a 'goal' than a bucket list item. The lines there are blurry, anyway. Don't worry that you don't have time or can't afford it or allow in any other negative thoughts. Don't worry if it seems too exotic, or conversely, too mundane. If it lights a fire in your belly, then it is perfect. Don't think it is not possible. If someone else in the world has done it, it is possible.

Get it down!

If it helps, write a 'NOT bucket list'. For instance, I will never do a bungy jump. Put that over to one corner of the page. Writing a NOT bucket list will help you clear the way for what you do want.

Finally, remember at this point that this does not have to look pretty. We will tidy it up later.

Aim for 100 items.

This may seem like a lot but it is not really. Remember the number of items on your bucket list doesn't really matter, but it is nice to have something to aim for.

Don't come back and do Step Two until you have got 100 items written down.

You have thirty minutes.

Go!

WORKBOOK NOTE

At the end of the chapter there will be a small area to write down any 'NOT bucket list' items followed by a list of 100 blank lines so you can write out the first draft of your bucket list.

Step Two: Questions and Prompts

Questions and prompts help you to figure out more bucket list items and also focus on finding items more attuned to you. Using questions has been found to have a massive impact because if a question is asked, even if it is not spoken aloud, your mind is still compelled to answer it.

There are four general areas of questions. You don't have to answer all these questions. They are just there as prompts so you can add to your brand new, 100-item bucket list, or to refine it so it reflects YOU.

Workbook Note

There are lines under the questions below to write your answers. Then if anything prompts a specific bucket list item, write it on the bucket list template at the end of the chapter.

Santa's Knee Questions

These come in various forms, but overall they help you think like an excited five-year-old sitting on Santa's knee. There are no filters, no limits, no boundaries. Go wild, go crazy. Ask for the impossible. For example:

- What would you like if there were no financial limits?
- What would you do if you had unlimited time, money and resources?
- If you won a huge lottery, what would you do (after you paid off the mortgage)?
- If fear were not part of the equation what would you do?
- If you were given three wishes, what would you wish for (excluding world peace, of course)?
- What 'toy' or luxury item would you like to own or have, even for a day?

Deathbed Regrets Questions

These help you confront your own mortality. The traditional definition of a bucket list—a list of items to check off before you die—does that, but these really ram it home. For example:

- What would you like to have said about you in your eulogy?
- What do you absolutely HAVE to do before you die?
- What would be your biggest regret on your deathbed?
- What would you do, see, or have if you only had one day to live?
- What would you do, see, or have if you only had 30 days to live?
- What would you do, see, or have if you only had one year to live?
- What would you do, see, or have if you only had five years to live?

_____

_____

_____

PASSIONS AND INTERESTS QUESTIONS

These help you to remember what you have always liked to do, or thought you would be good at but then decided that time, money or something else was in the way. These can be one-off things or longer-term hobbies. For example:

- What was your childhood dream to do, see, create?
- What have you always wanted to do that you felt like you didn't time for?
- What do you want to buy or do just to have fun?
- What would you do even without pay?
- What activity makes you lose track of time or gets you in a flow state?
- What has always been one of your biggest dreams in life?
- What would be a perfect day for you?

_____

_____

_____

_____

_____

Get Down to Specifics Questions

The next chapter contains a lot of help to refine your bucket list and answer some of your burning questions, like "Do I just write 'India' or 'Visit the Taj Mahal'?". But to give you a taster, here are some questions that can help you think about your new bucket list in alternative ways.

- What would you HAVE—buy or own?
- What would you DO—see or create?
- Where would you like to visit or travel—countries, places, locations?
- What new foods do you want to taste?
- Who do you want to meet in person?
- What experiences do you want to have?
- What activities do you want to try at least once?
- What activities or skills do you want to learn or master?
- What adventures would get you out of your comfort zone?
- What would you do in different seasons of the year?
- Are there any special moments or scheduled events you want to witness?

_____

_____

_____

_____

_____

_____

You Have a Bucket List!

This is the end of the main action-taking chapter. You have (at least) 100 bucket list items that make you smile, make your toes tingle and that make you want to jump out of bed in the morning.

They may be anything from silly little goals to epic adventures, crazy challenges or gentle achievements. The list is probably messy, in no particular order and you will have no idea how you would get even one item checked off, but you have your first draft bucket list!

If you haven't got 100 items yet, then don't worry; the next chapter helps you refine your personalized bucket list even more. It will also answer some of the questions that may have popped up during this two-part brainstorming and prompting exercise.

The 'NOT Bucket List'

Write down anything that you know will NOT be included on your bucket list here.

_____

_____

_____

_____

_____

_____

_____

JULIE SCHOOLER

BUCKET LIST

NAME _____

1 _____

2 _____

3 _____

4 _____

5 _____

6 _____

7 _____

8 _____

9 _____

10 _____

11 _____

12 _____

13 _____

14 _____

15 _____

Bucket List Blueprint WORKBOOK

16 _____

17 _____

18 _____

19 _____

20 _____

21 _____

22 _____

23 _____

24 _____

25 _____

26 _____

27 _____

28 _____

29 _____

30 _____

31 _____

32 _____

33 _____

34 ___
35 ___
36 ___
37 ___
38 ___
39 ___
40 ___
41 ___
42 ___
43 ___
44 ___
45 ___
46 ___
47 ___
48 ___
49 ___
50 ___
51 ___

Bucket List Blueprint WORKBOOK

52 _____

53 _____

54 _____

55 _____

56 _____

57 _____

58 _____

59 _____

60 _____

61 _____

62 _____

63 _____

64 _____

65 _____

66 _____

67 _____

68 _____

69 _____

70 _____

71 _____

72 _____

73 _____

74 _____

75 _____

76 _____

77 _____

78 _____

79 _____

80 _____

81 _____

82 _____

83 _____

84 _____

85 _____

86 _____

87 _____

88 _____

89 _____

90 _____

91 _____

92 _____

93 _____

94 _____

95 _____

96 _____

97 _____

98 _____

99 _____

100 _____

WHOOP WHOOP!

7
BUCKET LIST Q&A

 'Sometimes the questions are complicated and the answers are simple.' – Dr. Seuss

QUESTION AND ANSWER TIME

You now have 100 bucket list items scribbled down, and you are not sure what the heck you should do with the list. You are not even sure if it is 'right'. You are certainly not sure how you should begin crossing off the items, especially that super crazy 'fly into space' one. This chapter answers your burning questions about bucket lists and gives you some great tips so you can make your bucket list tidier AND more meaningful.

Q: I WAS HOPING FOR SOME IDEAS OR LISTS OF BUCKET LIST ITEMS. Can I look at the Internet now?

A: The brainstorm exercise purposely excluded use of the Internet, and there has been little reference to actual bucket list items up until this point so that you could tap into your own dreams and passions without being influenced by other people's ideas.

That said, there are some lists of bucket list items in the back of this book, including my Top40 Bucket List. And you can ask friends, use the Internet and get inspiration from all sorts of sources to add to your list. Now that you know how to tap into yourself, you will know upon seeing or hearing an idea if it is something you want to add to your list. Go check the Internet—I can't stop you from here!

Q: I AM NOT SURE IF THIS IS EVERYTHING I WANT TO DO. IS THIS A final list?

A: This bucket list is a first draft, a starting point. Your bucket list will evolve over the course of reading this book and then afterwards for the rest of your life. The most important thing is that you now have 100 items written down and that they are exciting and meaningful enough to you that you are willing to take action on them. That is it. The best bucket lists are simple and profound. Actually, I believe that the best things in life are both of those things, too.

Q: I HAVE WRITTEN SOME ITEMS DOWN, BUT I AM STILL NOT SURE IF they are what I really want—do I keep them on the list?

A: Short answer: YES. Like the first draft of anything, the first draft of your bucket list is not going to be your best work. You may not be sure if you want to take the item off because it is 'not really you' or because it suddenly seems too scary now that it is written down. Usually if it scares you, that is a good thing! So err on the side of caution and leave it on the list for now.

Q: How on earth am I going to get this entire list done?

A: You have time. You have the rest of your life! All you are doing at this stage is writing a list. Sure, scheduling items and putting deadlines in place plays a part—see Chapter Nine—but for now, don't worry.

> It is only a list of your most amazing dreams and deepest desires, nothing more (!).

One pro tip: stack or combine items. I wanted to attend an event, 'The World of Wearable Arts', which only happens in another city, Wellington. So I looked up other things to do in Wellington. I added 'Wellington Writers Walk' to my bucket list, and voila, two items that could be crossed off in the same weekend. Perhaps you want to learn to surf and do a meditation retreat? There are a number of places in Bali that offer both activities. Think 'stacking' when writing your list.

Please remember, you probably won't check off your entire bucket list in your lifetime, but that is not the point. Most people have no goals or only realistic goals. Be different. Set big, hairy audacious goals. Imagine a life in which half or a quarter or even one or two items are checked off—wouldn't it be far superior to the life you are currently living?

Q: I have written all this stuff down that I cannot afford or don't have time for, so where do I start?

A: The whole point of having a bucket list is to dream big but start small, and this will be detailed in Chapter Nine. For now, don't worry if you have written a big list of time consuming and expensive items. Writing an item down on your list is simply an acknowledgement that it is an item that you would like to tackle more than something that is not on your list.

> Writing a bucket list is supposed to be fun, not stressful!

Q: I THINK MY CHOICES ARE TOO MUNDANE. WHAT IF I DON'T WANT to do the travel or adventurous bucket list items?

A: Not everyone wants to ride in a hot air balloon over Cappadocia! Please do not worry if your choices don't seem exotic enough. A bucket list does not have to involve travel at all. You can take action on many items in your backyard. That is where I planted sunflower seeds and that is where I learned to juggle. Both are completely valid bucket list items.

Don't compare your bucket list to what you believe society thinks it should be. Most people will never have a bucket list, so who cares what they think, anyway? Modest goals you take action on are better than aspirational dreams you do nothing about.

One caveat to this—putting down items such as 'binge watch every episode of *Game of Thrones*' or 'get to the top level of a favorite computer game' is not really keeping with the essence of what a bucket list is about. Make your bucket list goals, however small, screen-free.

Q: I THINK MY CHOICES ARE TOO RISKY, HOW DO I KEEP SAFE?

A: This is a repeat of the disclaimer from the front of this book:

This book is designed to give the reader (that means YOU – the exceptionally awesome person reading this!) some useful tips and ideas about how to create and put into action your personal bucket list. It has suggestions for bucket list items, but every reader is ultimately responsible for selecting the items for his or her bucket list.

Bucket list items may pose some risk. The author and publisher advise readers to take full responsibility for their safety and know their limits. What this means for YOU:

- Talk to a health professional before embarking on any increased physical activity.

- Make sure you have full and correct insurance (travel, health, etc.) whenever required.
- Use common sense to keep safe when traveling locally or abroad and research safety measures that are appropriate in other countries or regions.
- Make sure any equipment you use has been well-maintained.
- Choose reputable companies with the best safety records.
- Tell someone where you are going, what you are doing, and when you expect to be back.
- Choose bucket list items that are within your means financially or for which you are prepared to budget and save.
- Make responsible arrangements so that your work, family and other important areas of life remain in good condition while you pursue your bucket list.

Please, please, please do not choose irresponsible, destructive or illegal items for your bucket list.

The author and publisher accept no responsibility for any harm or loss resulting from your pursuit of the bucket list. Have fun, but keep safe.

Q: I DON'T HAVE 100 ITEMS. SHOULD I KEEP TRYING FOR A BIGGER list?

A: You have permission to use the Internet now, so feel free to add items. That said, the length of the bucket list is not important. Starting one is. Some people have a handful of items, some have thousands. I would personally recommend an absolute minimum of 25, but again, this is not supposed to be overwhelming.

If you have a written list of items that you are happy with, then don't worry about how many there are. Once you start checking some off, you will see how addictive a bucket list is and come up with more ideas effortlessly. Doing some of the items leads to other similar items, and your bucket list gains momentum organically.

Q: I AM NOT SURE IF I HAVE WRITTEN MY BUCKET LIST 'RIGHT', ANY suggestions?

A: Write a bucket list item in a way that gives you the most powerful impact or highlights the essential parts of the item.

One way to do this is to get as specific as possible. Create a descriptive story in your head or on paper about the item with the sensations you want to experience. On the actual list you can use action words to reduce this down to a phrase that gets the essence of the item across. For instance, 'soaking in an infinity pool with a cocktail in my hand and the warmth of the sun on my face as I watch a gorgeous sunset' gets reduced to 'swim in an infinity pool'.

Work out the main non-negotiables of the bucket list item. Even though I know I want to experience many things on a future trip to France, I have simply written 'France – try Champagne in the Champagne district, visit Monet's garden, ride a bike through tiny French villages. This gets me excited and highlights the essential parts that will be fleshed out when I take action on this item in a few years.

The only other limitation on a bucket list is that it is not a goals list. Your goals can be professional or family oriented. Although a bucket list may overlap across other fields, it is more about finding things you have never done before, that are memorable and that will give you a deep satisfaction in doing or achieving.

A bucket list would not normally include a work goal such as moving to a new position. But it could be in the professional realm, such as writing a business book. It is not a habit such as exercising three times per week, but it could be a physical challenge such as winning a tennis tournament. It is not a resolution such as 'always be kind', but it could be a charitable challenge such as perform five random acts of kindness in a day.

If you are not sure if the item is a 'true' bucket list item or a life goal, don't worry. The fact that you have written it down means that, regardless of where it sits, it is more likely to happen. Some people would say, for instance, 'buying a house' is not a bucket list item but 'building a house' is. Bottom line is, it does not matter one iota. Get it down!

Q: THIS BUCKET LIST IS A MESS, IT IS NOT PRIORITIZED, AND I don't know where to start. Help!

A: This is your first draft bucket list. It is supposed to look messy. The next chapter will give you some ideas on how to organize and categorize your bucket list. This is completely optional, so feel free to skip that chapter if you are happy with how your list looks.

Q&A DELAY

Remember, just like the objections chapter, these questions are partly a delay attempt by your fearful mind to make you think you don't want to have a bucket list. Your thoughts could lead you to believe that writing down things that you may never get to do is pointless. But denying yourself the dream of swimming in infinity pools or cycling through tiny French villages is just as intolerable.

A bucket list is fun, but it takes time and effort and so it is hard work. Not having a bucket list, a chance to dream, is a painful, unsatisfactory and hard way to live. Choose your hard.

If you still want to delay taking action on your bucket list, or if you really want to tidy it up and get a bit more clarity around all the items, then the next chapter on categories and organization is for you. If you want to leap into actually checking off your first item, then skip to Chapter Nine.

HALF-WAY POINT CHECK IN

Note down any additional thoughts and ideas here.

8
ORGANIZE YOUR BUCKET LIST

 'A place for everything and everything in its place.' – Benjamin Franklin

A MAJOR ACHIEVEMENT

Congratulations on your brand new written down bucket list! Feel proud, as most people never write their bucket lists down. Feel excited as you are connecting into long-held dreams. And feel positive as you are focusing on things you really want to do.

This chapter is completely optional. You definitely do not have to organize your list in any way. You can just have a straight list that is in no particular order. Just writing a list is a major achievement. Pat yourself on the back and move on to the next chapter. But if you like the idea of organizing your list into common areas, this chapter is for you.

These ideas to categorize your bucket list are meant to be a help, not a hindrance. Please don't let this chapter overwhelm you as you are not sure what category to place items in or you haven't thought of items in a particular category. You don't need items in every category! One or two categories may be really long and others have only a handful of items. If re-organizing your list prompts you to think of more items, change items or even remove items, it is actually a good extra function of categorization.

Think of this chapter as an extra tool that can make your bucket list better. It is simply a way to structure your list in a way that may help it to make more sense to you. But if you don't want to take on the suggestions, please leave this tool in the toolbox for now.

Most importantly, don't let the suggestions here distract you from the goal of checking off items. Spend a little time organizing your bucket list and then move on to the next chapter. That is where the real magic happens.

Your Choice

There are a number of ways to categorize your bucket list. There are a few different approaches outlined below plus a suggested template. Most websites on bucket lists also have good category ideas, especially www.bucketlist.org. There is a list of websites in the References section at the end of the book.

The first way to organize your list is to go through the items and find any patterns or themes in them that naturally group them together. You can be quite general or specific here. You could include subcategories. You may want to rank the items or organize them along a time continuum. Of course, there will likely be crossover between categories, but just try to slot them into one place. For example, 'Dining at the top of the Eiffel Tower' — is that 'Travel' or 'Food' related? Whatever makes the most sense to you.

Note that alongside the different category templates, there will be a few examples of bucket list items. Feel free to add them to your bucket list if they speak to you.

Possible Category Templates

You could organize your list with some sort of time reference. For example, split items into the different seasons. Another way is to distinguish 'event specific' versus 'anytime' items. Some items, like concerts and festivals, will only be possible on specific dates and some, like indoor rock climbing, can be scheduled year-round. Or you could rank items in relation to when you want to do them, such as this month, this year, the next two years, five years, ten years, etc.

You may notice that items easily fall into the different senses. Or perhaps separate challenges into mental versus physical. For instance, solve a Rubik's cube versus do a triathlon. Travel items could be grouped into local, national and international categories.

Bucket list items could be spaced on a continuum from try out once to master a skill, leisurely to more adventurous or cheaper to expensive.

For example:

- Try out versus master: try playing a ukulele, learn the guitar, play in a rock band
- Leisurely to more adventurous: fly in a seaplane, fly in an aerobatic plane, fly in a fighter jet
- Cheaper to more expensive: ride on a hired tandem bike, do a tandem skydive

Another way to view your bucket list is to tag what you would like to do by yourself versus with others—partners, kids and friends. More on this in Chapter Ten.

Suggested Category Template

My top favorite category template is an acronym that spells 'BUCKET'.

Here it is:

B – Buy
U – Undertakings
C – Create
K – Kindness
E – Experiences
T – Travel

This is what the categories mean:

B – Buy – Material items you want to buy or own
U – Undertakings – Things to learn or master, or challenges you want to do
C – Create – Stuff you want to make or build or that will use your creativity
K – Kindness – Items with a charitable focus or kind acts for others
E – Experiences – Adventurous pursuits, fun activities or exciting experiences
T – Travel – Anything travel and tourism related

Here is the 'BUCKET' category system using examples from my Top40 Bucket List:

B – Buy- Hanging 'egg' chair
U – Undertakings- Write a novel in a month
C – Create- Plant and grow sunflowers
K – Kindness- N/A
E – Experiences- Ride on a jet ski, try curling
T – Travel- Fly to Queenstown for a burger

Here is the 'BUCKET' category system using other examples:

B – Buy- A vintage airplane, stamp collection
U – Undertakings- Learn to tango, learn Spanish
C – Create- Knit a scarf, write a song
K – Kindness- Give blood, work in a soup kitchen
E – Experiences- Go on a trapeze, cuddle a lion cub
T – Travel- Raft the Grand Canyon, visit Hawaii

As you see from the examples above, you do not have to place items in every category. I purposely didn't put any charity or community focused items on my Top40 Bucket List as I give in other ways.

You will also notice that it is sometimes still hard to classify items. Fly to Queenstown for a burger. Is that more 'Travel' or 'Experiences'? Ultimately, any classification is at your discretion.

Even though there are some downsides to this particular template, I love this as it is easy to remember, it is wide enough to capture almost every bucket list item imaginable, and it organizes items into intuitively decipherable categories.

Of course, there may be some that don't easily fall into a one of the spots or could be cross categorized, but that will occur with any attempt to structure your bucket list.

ADDITIONAL TRAVEL CATEGORY TEMPLATE

Depending on how many travel related items you have on your bucket list, you may want to subcategorize the 'Travel' category.

I didn't need to do this with my Top40 Bucket List as I only had a few travel items. However, I have created a handy template that you are welcome to use.

And, of course, it is an acronym of the word 'TRAVEL:

T – Transport- Use of planes, trains, bikes, ships, etc.
R – Restaurants and Food- Restaurants, food or drink from places or cultures
A – Activities and Adventure- Fun or exciting endeavors
V – Visit- Places to visit and sightsee
E – Experiences and Events- Booked experiences or date specific events
L – Lodging- Accommodation and places to stay

Here are some examples of items that fall into the 'TRAVEL' template:

T – Transport- Ride on the Orient Express, drive Route 66
R – Restaurants and Food- Eat at a Michelin star restaurant, try fried crickets
A – Activities and Adventure- Dogsled in Alaska, swim with whales in Tonga
V – Visit- Go to the Galapagos Islands, see Niagara Falls
E – Experiences and Events- Attend Burning Man festival, visit Dollywood
L – Lodging- Stay at the Ice Hotel, stay in a Scottish castle

Notice that some items are specific to a place and other ideas can happen in different parts of the world. Again, it may be hard to choose which category an item falls into.

Deciding what is an 'Adventure', what is a 'Visit' and what is an 'Experience' may be difficult at times. Is going to Dollywood an adventure, a visit or an experience? Just go with your gut and place it based on your first instinctive decision.

In Appendix Two there are a few more examples of bucket list items that use the 'BUCKET' and 'TRAVEL' category templates to give you an even better understanding of categorization.

CATEGORIZE QUICKLY AND MOVE ON

This chapter is a way to make your bucket list more manageable so you don't feel overloaded with 100 items in a long list. If doing this does overwhelm you, then stop! Keep your file just as it is.

But if you have found a category system that works for you or you are using the 'BUCKET' and 'TRAVEL' templates, then quickly rewrite your list.

In either case, the most important step is to move onto the next chapter. This is where you get to finally take action on that first bucket list item.

CATEGORIZE YOUR BUCKET LIST

If it helps, use the category templates below to categorize your Bucket list.

BUCKET

    B – Buy
    U – Undertakings
    C – Create
    K – Kindness
    E – Experiences
    T – Travel

_____

_____

_____

_____

_____

TRAVEL

T – Transport
R – Restaurants and Food
A – Activities and Adventure
V – Visit
E – Experiences and Events
L – Lodging

_____

_____

_____

_____

_____

OTHER CATEGORIES

_____

_____

_____

_____

_____

9
CHECK OFF THE FIRST BUCKET LIST ITEM

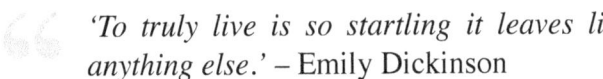
'To truly live is so startling it leaves little time for anything else.' – Emily Dickinson

IT IS ACTION TIME

You have a bucket list of at least 25 and preferably 100 (or even more) items. It may be in categories or simply be a straight list. You are happy with the list, it feels like 'you', and it is complete for now.

This chapter is about how to get your list into a format that you will read on a regular basis and then put into action. By the end of this chapter you will have done at least one item on your list. It is very important to get the feeling of achievement that comes with actually checking a bucket list item off, as that creates a drive to do more of the items.

It's time to stop 'listing' and start living!

Display and Read Your Bucket List

If your bucket list has been done with pen and paper, I recommend creating a digital version of the list, whether in a Word document, typed in an email to yourself or in a notes app on your phone, just so you have another copy of it somewhere.

Make sure you have your first, finalized version of your bucket list somewhere you have easy access to it and see it every day. Use the pen and paper version or print it out and stick it to your wall, on the fridge, on the bathroom mirror, or for those who are more private, inside the door to your wardrobe. Or tuck it into a journal you write in regularly.

If you have an electronic Word document or PDF of your bucket list, then place that document on your computer desktop, or add it into your notes or books apps on your phone.

Some of you who are more public may want to share your bucket list on your favorite social media feed, on Pinterest or on your own blog. Sharing it and getting others involved keeps you even more accountable, but it may not be for everyone. More on this soon.

A fun but completely optional way to display your bucket list is to create a 'vision board' from it. A vision board is any sort of board on which you display images that represent your bucket list items — what you want to do, see and have in life.

Create one the old-fashioned way out of cut outs from magazines stuck to a big piece of paper or cardboard. Or combine some pictures into an online board on Pinterest or elsewhere.

An extra cool idea is to take a photo of your written bucket list or its physical vision board and upload it so it becomes your computer screen saver or wallpaper on your phone.

Choose to display your bucket list in a way that reflects you. Don't spend days and days on this point as it can easily turn into a procrastination attempt. The point is to not forget your bucket list. Look at it, refer to it and read it often. It will become more real the more you review it and then you are more likely to take action with it.

Schedule Your Dreams

So far, you have been asked to dream big. Now it is time to schedule your dreams. You have a bucket list somewhere handy. Now scan through the list and find TWO items you can put in your diary, calendar or online scheduling program. How you schedule things, on a digital system or physically written down, is not important. What is important is getting them in the diary.

Choose the FIRST item that you can check off quickly. Think LOW COST or LOCAL or LITTLE TIME. As part of the Top40 Bucket List, I decided to try curling. I found a local ice-skating rink and went to their Sunday night one-hour long tryout session for $10. It was kind of fun and kind of a challenge and I bruised my knee badly, but that is not the point. I checked off that bucket list item relatively easily as it was low cost, local and took little time.

Choose a SECOND item that will take some planning in terms of expense, research or resources required. Around the same time I checked off 'try curling' from my bucket list, I started planning the trip to Wellington for 'The World of Wearable Arts' event that was happening later in the year. I looked up tickets, airfares and accommodation and started booking them.

It doesn't matter what day or time you put the item in, or whether you think you will be able to do it; just scheduling it gives it a lot of power, almost a life of its own.

If you have to reschedule it, fine. But it will always be in your diary until you have taken action on it.

MY FIRST BUCKET LIST ITEM IS...

_____

_____

_____

MY SECOND BUCKET LIST ITEM IS...

_____

_____

_____

Why Starting Small Works

The way to start your bucket list is to start small. Check one 'easy win' item off and do little things (look up flights, etc.) on the bigger things.

This low-hanging fruit starts building your 'bucket list action taker' muscle. The happy feeling of checking things off, even the small things, makes you feel like your bucket list is achievable. By DOING, you change your beliefs on what you think you can do. This creates excitement, a fire in your belly, a reason to spring out of bed in the morning.

You may have thought there was a one-way street between thought and behavior. You smile because you are happy. But that is not always the case. Think about the times you make yourself smile even when you are not feeling that happy. Does your body make you think you are a bit happier simply by smiling?

Bucket List Blueprint WORKBOOK

The same analogy applies to taking action on your bucket list. Doing one thing, anything at all, interrupts your normal thought patterns and makes you think that these previously impossible things are now possible. Utilize the power of DOING and see how much your beliefs around acting on your long-held dreams change.

When I wrote out my Top40 Bucket List, there were a number of LOW COST or LOCAL or LITTLE TIME items. I did many of these in the first few months of the year. It gave me a handful of small successes and made me think checking off the entire 40 items in a year would be achievable.

Six items I did early on: planting sunflower seeds, trying a gourmet ice-cream place, starting a memory jar with my four-year-old, trying stand up paddle boarding, trying a rosé wine ice-block and trying curling cost less than $50 in total. All together they gave me a huge boost in confidence that I could tackle some of the more daunting and expensive items such as a hot air balloon ride and a tandem sky dive.

ACCOUNTABILITY

Writing a bucket list, reading it and even scheduling items may not be enough to actually do them. It can be a good idea to add some accountability to your bucket list.

Now, some of you may not want to tell the world about your deepest desires, and that is perfectly valid. You may be worried that others will tell you that what you want to do is impossible. You may not want to set yourself up to fail in public. And you may not want people to think you are being selfish or crazy. As we have discussed, most people will never attempt to have a bucket list so their reactions do not matter. However, keep your bucket list private for now if that feels right for you.

If you want to go public it is super easy these days. Paste your bucket list online everywhere and tell your friends about it. Update your Facebook, Instagram or Pinterest presence with photos of your bucket list wins. Ask your friends and family to join you in some of the experiences you want to do. And don't be afraid to ask for their help to check off items.

When I decided on my wacky endeavor to do 40 bucket list items in a year, I asked friends for their suggestions. Some ideas were exactly what I would like to do, but they had to go on a long-term bucket list due to financial or logistic constraints.

One thing I really wanted to do but had no idea if it was possible was to fly an hour and a half to Queenstown to eat a burger from an infamous burger joint called FergBurger, which serves such amazing burgers that it always has a line of hungry people snaking down the block. It ended up making the Top40 cut thanks to two friends. One friend was happy to come with me on the adventure and had air points to use up, and another friend happened to have just moved to Queenstown and could pick us up from the airport and take us to the burger place. This made it both financially and logistically possible. In the fresh air of Queenstown, under the stunning vista of the surrounding mountains, that was, without doubt, the best burger I have ever eaten.

Use Deadlines

Another way to stay accountable, if only to yourself, is to create deadlines. Some items will naturally have limited times. For instance, if you want to see a particular artist in concert, go to a specific festival or see a seasonal or natural wonder like the Northern Lights or an eclipse.

Sometimes, however, deadlines are completely artificial but are strong enough to be an inspiration. I set a goal to check 40 things off my bucket list during the calendar year of 2016. I jumped out of a plane on the 30th of December 2016, one day before my deadline. Yes, it was self-imposed. And no one else would care if I jumped out on the 1st of January 2017. But I would. As I had completed the rest of the list and there was a deadline looming, completing the jump became more important than the fear.

Referring to your bucket list regularly, scheduling items, starting small, telling people your intentions and using deadlines are fantastic ways to make your bucket list happen. Together they create an enormously powerful force that makes it almost impossible not to take action.

ACTION TIME

Pick out one item from your bucket list that you can do in the next week. Think LOW COST or LOCAL or LITTLE TIME (or all three). Get excited, get ready and get it done.

MY FIRST BUCKET LIST ITEM IS...

_____

_____

_____

MY SECOND BUCKET LIST ITEM IS...

_____

_____

_____

10
BUCKET LISTS WITH FAMILY AND FRIENDS

'Life isn't about waiting for the storm to pass; it's about learning to dance in the rain.' – Vivian Greene

SHARING IS CARING

Up until now you will be forgiven for thinking that creating a bucket list is a very individual endeavor. This book has focused on the bucket list you create being personal and related to your dreams and passions. The items are things you want to do, regardless of whether anyone else is interested.

But where is the fun in that? There is nowhere near as much joy in completing your bucket list items by yourself, as there is in including others.

You may object to this, as it is not their bucket list. And yes, you are right. But a large portion of the population will never create their own bucket lists. Most people are usually quite happy to hop on board when someone is planning something fun or exciting. If you show yourself as a leader in this area, you are likely to find someone you know who will join you when you embark on your next crazy idea.

Although I was happy to do all of my Top40 Bucket List items on my own, in the end I only did nine of the 40 by myself. From stand up paddle boarding, to curling, to even that daunting tandem skydive, I had a friend who was happy to join me. In the case of 'Drunk Shopping', which was officially my 40th birthday celebration, I had a whole bunch of friends who were happy to have a few glasses of wine over lunch and then go shopping. So. Much. Fun!

PARTNERS

If you have a special someone in your life, creating a bucket list is a perfect way to spend quality time with him or her. Your loved one can tag along on your bucket list ideas, or—even better—you can both create a list and decide on your favorite ideas that you would like to do together.

Other than the obvious of not being alone, there are a ton of benefits of marking off bucket list items with your other half. Doing things together strengthens a relationship, as there are usually positive memories associated with the task. You can reminisce with your partner about the time you visited Tuscany and made pasta from scratch or kissed under that waterfall you hiked to last summer.

If you like to do more adventurous things together, then it has been shown in dating experiments that anything that makes the heart race increases attractiveness between couples. There is a theory that even though the heart is racing due to the activity, the mind can easily believe it is due to the allure of the other person. And in other studies, it has been proven that couples in long-term relationships feel more attracted to each other when they regularly engage in novel and exciting activities that involve working together to achieve a goal, for example, building a tree house together.

Most things on a bucket list are adaptable for two people, but some ideas are especially suitable for couples. Great ideas specifically for twosomes include doing a tandem bike ride together, dance lessons, mastering your chess game, trying indoor rock climbing, or anything that seems romantic like a couples massage, sunset watching or dinner at a Michelin star restaurant.

BUCKET LIST IDEAS - PARTNER

_____

_____

_____

_____

_____

_____

CHILDREN

No matter how old your children are, a bucket list can bring about unforgettable experiences and cherished family memories. Again, like couples, you could bring the kids along for the ride on your own bucket list or invite them to think of items and create a family list. Kids, once prompted, are very good at this exercise. They will have a wish list a mile long before you know it.

Whichever way you choose to do this depends on how old your kids are and whether they are enthusiastic about your ideas already. But just making a family bucket list together—before you check anything off—is helpful for connecting on a higher level with your tiny humans.

There are lots of benefits when the whole family is involved with checking off a bucket list. Your kids gain important life skills such as persistence, making decisions and tackling risk in a controlled environment with a parent around. They learn to make goals and achieve them, and they grow less fearful and more confident as a result. Just like you, they have to move away from their usual comfort zones and add some variety and adventure into their young lives. If travel outside of your local area is involved, they may get a better understanding of other cultures and gain empathy for different people they meet.

Also, you bond more with your kids as you share common fears, struggles and obstacles. Even if you end up doing the actual item by yourself (like running a marathon, for example), they can come with you on training runs and cheer from the sidelines on the big day. And if they are fully involved (like mastering a card trick or building a go-cart together), this can only enhance the strong relationship you already have.

> If nothing else, it gets your kids and you off screens and into real life—and everyone can agree that that is a wonderful thing.

One bucket list idea specifically designed with kids in mind is creating a memory jar. A memory jar is simply any jar or box that gets filled up with little notes about fun family times you have done together. So on your bucket list you can write 'create a memory jar' and when you complete items from your bucket list, you can write a little note or draw a picture, or keep the ticket stub, etc., and add it to the jar.

This is kind of meta, but also cheap and easy, plus it helps your children savor the experience even more. More about savoring in the next chapter as a good way of enhancing your bucket list experience. Similar to the memory jar idea, you can create a time capsule or a treasure chest as a family.

Bucket List Blueprint WORKBOOK

Other (mostly very low cost) ideas with kids include playing a round of disc (Frisbee) golf, trying to catch a fish (e.g.: from a wharf), learning to juggle, performing a magic trick, making a pottery bowl, knitting a scarf, folding origami into a special design, going ice-skating, planting a tree or putting a message in a bottle and throwing it out to sea together.

This is just the tip of the iceberg to give a flavor of cheap, cool things that will bring you together as a family, keep the kids off the screens, and give you all positive memories that will last a lifetime.

BUCKET LIST IDEAS - CHILDREN

_____

_____

_____

_____

_____

_____

_____

FRIENDS

As already noted, a bucket list item is usually enhanced with a friend or two joining you. I know I wouldn't have enjoyed the hot air balloon ride or the tandem skydive as much if it weren't for a brave friend, in each of the experiences, who said that they were keen to join me.

But the power of bucket lists can really be seen if a big group of you gets together and does something. If you want to build a house for charity, for example, then this is much better when you can rope in a whole bunch of buddies who can help. Sharing the joy of achieving a big goal makes it even better.

Other bucket list ideas that really lend themselves to bigger groups or require some help and support include: throwing a surprise party, attempting to break a Guinness World Record, going to a music festival or creating a flash mob. And if you have ever wanted to get hold of one of those enormous bottles of champagne so you could shower it everywhere, it is much better if you have some friends around who have 'get soaked with champagne' on their bucket lists.

Really, almost every bucket list item you can imagine with the possible exception of learning to ride a unicycle (but even then a steady hand from another person may be useful) is better with someone else. So share your bucket list with your friends and family. You may be surprised to find out that some latent dreams that your nearest and dearest have been harboring are already on your bucket list, and you are a catalyst for them finally taking action.

BUCKET LIST IDEAS - FRIENDS

_____

_____

_____

_____

_____

_____

Checking off your bucket list with friends and family is a great way to supercharge it, to enhance the positive attributes of it. But it is not the only way. The next chapter shows how you can get the most out of your bucket list.

11
SUPERCHARGE YOUR BUCKET LIST

 'It's kind of fun to do the impossible.' – Walt Disney

MAGNIFY YOUR HAPPINESS

You may be feeling fairly sorted and settled on your bucket list, especially now that you have checked off at least one thing. This is fun! This is doable! This is making me feel awesome!

Now, in this penultimate chapter, you have the option of making your bucket list even more amazing by directly connecting it to proven drivers for happiness.

If you are content with how your bucket list is tracking right now, feel free to disregard this chapter. However, all these ideas magnify the happiness that you can extract from your bucket list, so they are worth noting.

Have a quick peek at the following five suggestions and see if any resonate with you.

1. Create a Challenge Around Your Bucket List

As I have been describing all the way through this book, in 2016, the year I turned 40, I wrote down 40 things I wanted to do, see, experience or have within the 12 months from January to December. I called this my 'Top40 Bucket List'. To cut a long story short—yes—I did take action on every single Top40 bucket list item and managed to complete them in the 12 months, with just a day to spare when I jumped out of a plane on the 30th of December 2016.

It was hard work! I definitely made some mistakes and had some issues. Technically, three items were not done properly, but I did at least try them or start them. I should have done some more items earlier in the year over summertime instead of leaving them right to the end. And by procrastinating on the tandem skydive, even though it was a spectacular way to finish off the Top40, I let it create a lot of fear in my mind. I should have gotten it done earlier.

I sure wish I'd had a book just like this one to refer to when I decided to embark on this crazy challenge.

But even though it was hard, it was without doubt one of the best experiences of my entire life. Up there with my wedding and the birth of my children. Setting a 'BHAG' – a big, hairy, audacious goal, and then actually achieving it makes me feel proud, improves my self-esteem and makes me believe I can be a better person.

> By exceeding what I thought my potential was, by seeing that I was only limited by my own beliefs, I feel like I am in an excellent position to tackle further challenges and smash through fears.

It may seem like creating a bucket list is enough of a challenge, but if you amp it up—do so many items in a year, or before you turn a certain age, or add items that you are very fearful of or that really challenge and stretch you—I guarantee you will feel even more happy and fulfilled.

Bucket List Blueprint WORKBOOK

Trying to mark off bucket list items is hard. Adding a crazy challenge to your bucket list project that will make you feel more fulfilled and happy but also increases the risk of failure is hard. Choose your hard.

2. BE GRATEFUL

Being grateful creates awareness of the good in your life. Gratitude studies have shown that an appreciation practice is associated with being more enthusiastic about life, being interested in the community, being kinder to others and getting better sleep, among a myriad of other positive outcomes.

Being thankful for knowing you can create a bucket list, feeling appreciative when writing down some of your dreams and then feeling gratitude when you check off some of the items can enhance your bucket list experience tremendously.

There is a deceptively simple but powerful exercise called 'Three Good Things'. Use it whenever you are taking action on your bucket list and multiply your happiness. You can also do this exercise at the end of the day about anything in your life, not just your bucket list, as a daily gratitude practice.

Three Good Things:

1. List ONE good or happy thing from your day.
2. Write it down, tell your partner or speak the answer out loud to yourself.
3. Ask yourself WHY it happened—what was it about YOU (your character, personality, traits, strengths, qualities or skills, etc.) that helped it to occur.
4. Take a few moments to feel good about yourself—SAVOR that positive feeling.
5. Do this whole exercise again for TWO more things if you have time.

Three Good Things Exercise

Write down three good things and detail what it was about YOU that helped them to happen.

_____

_____

_____

_____

_____

_____

_____

For example, I looked up the best and most scenic places to safely bicycle around in France today. This helped me take one step towards my future trip to France that I wrote down on my bucket list. Feeling excited about planning this trip will make it easy for me to start saving for it.

It is not the good thing that is important but the connection to you, that third step, that is the supercharging mechanism. Step three focuses on your role in creating that good thing and gets you thinking about specific positive traits in YOU that contributed to the happy moment.

Over time you see that you have control over creating these happy experiences, and your positive outlook starts to be imbedded in your identity. So you get to feed your need for certainty and transform your identity, two of the most powerful drivers of your life. The savoring step simply locks in all the goodness from the whole exercise.

3. Savor the Experience

Positive psychologists, researchers whose focus is happiness and other positive emotional states, describe three tiers to happiness: living a pleasurable life, a good life and a meaningful life. All three of these tiers can be applied to bucket lists.

Check back at those 'deathbed regret' questions that prompted you to think of bucket list items. They asked what you would do, see or have with one day, 30 days, one year or five years to live. Very loosely, the shorter time periods can correspond to a pleasurable life and the longer ones to a good or meaningful life.

One criticism of a bucket list is that is just a pleasant distraction from normal life. And perhaps it is. But even if you choose just 'pleasurable' activities and not ones that are related to what positive psychologists call a 'good' or 'meaningful' life, your bucket list items will still serve a greater purpose than being a frivolous diversion.

But only if you **savor** them. Savoring, or its synonyms, luxuriating, reveling, marveling, relishing or basking are easy methods of finding pleasure in everyday moments.

So while you are in the middle of your bucket list item, really take it in, be completely mindful of the moment, even for a few seconds. Let your brain absorb and relish in this positive activity. Try to be fully present.

If you forget at the time, you can savor an experience you have not done yet. In fact, one of the main reasons to write a bucket list is to get you excited about doing the things on it. In other words, you can still live a pleasurable life even if you are future oriented. Studies have proven that planning, researching and looking forward to experiences creates almost as much happiness as the experience itself. This seems to only apply to experiences and not material purchases. Sometimes the best laid plans may have to be cancelled last minute, but that doesn't necessarily counter the days, weeks or months of happy anticipation you already had.

Probably the best way to savor your bucket list is to create ways to remember all the tasks you have completed. You can bask in the past. You can take photos of each one and put them in a special 'Bucket List Album' (digital or physical). You can share what you did with others. Or you can create a box of keepsakes or a memory jar as described previously. If your bucket list involves a lot of travel, perhaps getting a world map and dotting it with pins of places you have been to is a good way to savor your experiences. There are many options, but please find some way to congratulate yourself and celebrate every single item.

4. Link Your Bucket List Items to Your Strengths

Although the pleasures in life—especially if you are mindful of them—will give you a pleasurable life, there is another level that gives you 'a good life'. This is where you use your strengths and abilities to work towards something, create something or improve yourself.

Checking off a bucket list is a perfect opportunity to try something new, challenge yourself with a task or attempt to master something. In other words, it enables you to use your strengths and abilities to attain 'a good life'. Try to ensure you have at least a few items that involve personal effort. For example, training to run a marathon, learning a new language or reconditioning an old classic car.

If you want mostly fun and pleasurable activities on your bucket list, then by all means focus on that first tier of happiness. No judgment here! There is no mandate to add in these pursuits that may not make you feel good at first, but help you grow as a person. But once you have satiated yourself on the pleasures in life, consider adding in a couple of challenges to your bucket list. You may be surprised about how fulfilled they make you feel.

When I participated in National Novel Writing Month (NaNoWriMo) as part of my Top40 Bucket List, writing 50,000 words (equivalent of a 200-page book) in a month seemed daunting.

It was, surprisingly, a massive happiness boost as the challenge pushed me to enhance my existing writing skills, tap into my creativity and overall grow as a person. It doesn't matter that the silly romance novel I wrote is sitting in the proverbial bottom drawer and is unlikely to be published, the challenge in itself was extremely rewarding.

Remember back in Chapter Four when the need for growth was discussed as a critical need that many people diminish as other needs take priority? Adding challenges to your bucket list that require you to develop existing abilities or master new skills fulfills this deep need for growth in a positive way.

5. Bring More Meaning to Your Bucket List

A bucket list improves your life, makes you happier and therefore contributes to a better world. But for some of you, this still won't be enough of a reason to create one. You need something more.

The ultimate aim is not only to live a pleasurable life or good life but a **meaningful** life. You attain a meaningful life from a connection to a wider cause. In other words, from fulfilling your need for contribution. The positive psychologists and personal development gurus have intersected here again, both with an emphasis on giving.

You certainly do not have to add any item onto your bucket list that involves charitable work, but for some, this will add a layer of meaning to their bucket list. In fact, I don't recommend it at all unless you feel like you have something to give. And the best way to do that is to feel fulfilled yourself before you give, so do some of your own personal dream items from your bucket list first.

Once you have checked off a few 'fill your own cup' items, feel free to add and take action on items such as 'work in a soup kitchen for a day' or 'bake cupcakes for the local rest home', or 'help build a school in a developing country'.

A fun way to gain meaning from your bucket list is to add an item such as 'do five random acts of kindness in one day' or 'do one random act of kindness per day for a month'. You can get lots of ideas from randomactsofkindness.org.

For instance, offer a glass of water to the package delivery person, leave some extra coins in the parking meter or send a friend a bunch of flowers out of the blue. It has been proven that doing five acts of kindness in a single day gives a significant boost to happiness — maybe a new idea to try out as a part of a family bucket list?

And yes, helping others to achieve their bucket list dreams is an extremely satisfying way to add more meaning to your bucket list. Ask people what would be their ultimate dreams and help them to step out of their comfort zones.

Be a leader, be a friend.

Supercharging Options

These high-level suggestions to supercharge your bucket list are all optional. Just reading this book and writing out some bucket list items may be enough for you right now.

Please remember to read this chapter when you are a little further along in your bucket list project. It may prompt you to add a challenge, remember to feel gratitude, savor your experiences, or add items that will extend you as a person or bring even more meaning into your life.

Next, the final chapter is a wrap up of the main take home points of this book.

How will you supercharge your bucket list?

Write down the supercharging ideas from above that resonate most with you and add in any of your own.

12

BUCKET LIST WRAP UP

 'To live is the rarest thing of all. Most people exist, that is all.' – Oscar Wilde

THE SIX HUMAN NEEDS (AGAIN)

Look at what you have accomplished with reading this book—you not only have a bucket list of 100 items that reflects your deepest desires and long-held dreams, but you have checked off one or more items on it already.

Many, many people in this world cannot fathom the amazing feeling you can invoke from writing down a goal and then taking action to achieve it. Not only do you now know what that feeling is like, you also know exactly how to get it back again, over and over, by checking off more bucket list items.

Remember that feeling of certainty we all crave at the deepest level? As you can now see, ironically you can get that exact feeling —feeling secure in yourself because you are in charge of your life —by increasing the level of variety in your life. That is, by meeting your need for certainty, through taking action systematically on your bucket list, you also get to meet one of your other main needs, the need for variety.

All of your other needs are also met through writing down a personalized bucket list and taking action on it. You meet your need for significance, as you know most people never attempt to write a bucket list and even fewer take action with it. You also meet your need for love as you often attain your bucket list items with your family and friends and so strengthen your relationships with them. And of course, you learn about yourself and set challenges to master skills and so meet your need for growth. Plus, if you add a few community-minded ventures onto your list you can meet your need for contribution. What other tool can help meet so many needs—in a positive way—at the same time?

A Mere Tool

A bucket list is not just a nice thing to have; it is a necessary part of a satisfying life, as shown by the fact that it meets all your deepest human needs.

But it is still only a tool.

In fact, although this whole book has been about creating and taking action on your bucket list, the main message is to get you to focus and decide what you really want in life. The bucket list is simply an instrument to help you understand yourself better, reconnect with your innermost desires and take action in spite of the fear.

This bucket list book has hopefully shown you that if you step out of your comfort zone to try something new, the world will not end.

You get to dance with fear instead of cowering from it.

Sure, you may not succeed, but trying and failing is always better than not trying because of the fear.

It is also about connecting with others. Getting you to do things out in the world that make you interact with other cultures and societies. Enabling you to simply have fun and complete challenges with loved ones—partners, kids, family and friends. No other factor in positive psychology research has been linked to increased happiness more than good, close, loving relationships, and a bucket list is a great facilitator in this regard.

Use this bucket list book, your own bucket list and your rediscovered ability to take action, to design the life you want, to have fun, to understand yourself better and to connect with others.

Isn't that what life is all about?

Simple Yet Powerful

You don't have to share your bucket list with anyone, and you don't have to invite friends and family to do it with you. Even if you keep your bucket list private, your loved ones will see a change in you. They will notice that you have more of a spring in your step as you focus on what you want, that you have a newfound zest for life and seem lighter and happier overall.

A good, well-written bucket list captures what you really want in life. In doing so, it will create an excitement deep in your soul that will easily lead you to living life to the fullest. It is an effortless way to invite energy and enthusiasm back into your life.

It is truly astounding that a simple list of goals and dreams can be the catalyst for a more fulfilling life. That all it takes to avoid those deathbed regrets is to tap into what you want and do something about it. But now that you have seen it and felt it.

You know deep down how powerful a bucket list can be.

The most important thing to remember with a bucket list is not to let it stagnate. Keep looking at it, adding to it, changing it, and most importantly, checking items off of it.

Don't be afraid to be spontaneous and be flexible. This is meant to be a long-term practice that will turn into a habit and be part of your lifestyle. The most important thing is to take action. Live.

Go and take a look at your bucket list right now and find another thing you can take action on before you close this book. Enquire about that salsa dancing class, ask for some vacation time for that multi-day hike or book in that Michelin star restaurant at its next available slot. Plant those sunflower seeds today.

It doesn't matter what you do, just that you do something.

MY NEXT BUCKET LIST ITEM IS...

BUCKET LIST BLUEPRINT WORKBOOK - ADDITIONAL NOTES

APPENDIX ONE – MY TOP40 BUCKET LIST

This is the approximate order in which I ended up checking off items.

1. Plant and grow sunflowers
2. Start a memory jar with Dylan
3. Eat an ice-cream at Giapo
4. Day trip to Rotoroa Island
5. Try stand up paddle boarding
6. Chef's Table Degustation
7. Try a glass of proper champagne
8. Fly to Queenstown for a burger
9. Try a rosé wine ice block
10. See Madonna in concert
11. Spend a weekend at Mangawhai
12. Try curling
13. Attend Auckland Writers Festival
14. Learn to juggle (still practicing)
15. Go on a wellness retreat
16. Try a powerhoop class
17. Own a Kindle Paperwhite

18. Create a print version of my eBook
19. Dye my hair a strange color – probably blue
20. Tony Robbins Seminar in Sydney
21. Girls weekend away
22. Wellington Writers Walk
23. World of Wearable Arts
24. Walk the Coast to Coast walkway from Auckland to Manukau
25. Fly in a seaplane
26. Get a blow wave at Dry and Tea
27. Liquid lunch and drunk shopping
28. Get a GHD super duper hairdryer
29. See a film in Gold Class
30. Ride on a tandem bike
31. Ride in/drive a Porsche or Aston Martin (sat in one)
32. Participate in NaNoWriMo – write a novel in a month
33. Buy an egg chair
34. Frisbee/Disc Golf
35. Ride on the back of a Harley Davidson
36. Ride in a hot air balloon
37. Publish at least one children's picture book (in progress)
38. Ride on a jet ski
39. Catch a fish (went fishing, nothing caught)
40. Tandem Skydive

APPENDIX TWO – A SELECTION OF BUCKET LIST IDEAS

Below is an assortment of four bucket list items slotted into each of the 'BUCKET' and 'TRAVEL' category templates.

The items hold no particular relevance and are in no order. They are simply meant to spark your own ideas.

Feel free to select from these lists for your own personal bucket list and organize them into categories as you see fit.

BUCKET

    B – Buy
    U – Undertakings
    C – Create
    K – Kindness
    E – Experiences
    T – Travel

Appendix Two – A Selection of Bucket List Ideas

Buy

- Vintage car
- Famous artwork
- Smart speaker (e.g.: Amazon Echo)
- Fitness and sleep tracker (e.g.: Fitbit)

Undertakings

- Break a world record
- Get a hole in one
- Finish a triathlon
- Master a magic trick

Create

- Knit a scarf
- Write a song
- Create a secret recipe
- Make and bury a time capsule

Kindness

- Give blood
- Visit your sponsor child
- Clean all the litter off one beach
- Volunteer in a homeless shelter for a day

Experiences

- Sumo suit wrestling
- Yoga retreat
- Get a tattoo
- Ride on a mechanical bull

Appendix Two – A Selection of Bucket List Ideas

TRAVEL

T – Transport
R – Restaurants and Food
A – Activities and Adventure
V – Visit
E – Experiences and Events
L – Lodging

Transport

- Ride in a sidecar of a motorcycle (Shanghai)
- Drive Route 66 (USA)
- Dogsledding (Alaska)
- Travel on the Orient Express (Europe)

Restaurants and Food

- Waste free restaurant (Melbourne)
- All glass undersea restaurant (Maldives)
- Michelin star restaurant (France)
- Try fried scorpion (Thailand)

Activities and Adventures

- Swim with whales (Tonga)
- Raft down the Grand Canyon (USA)
- Walk the Inca Trail to Machu Picchu (Peru)
- Take a trip into space

Visit

- Galapagos Islands
- Blue lagoon (Iceland)
- Game park animals (South Africa)
- Legoland (Denmark)

Appendix Two – A Selection of Bucket List Ideas

Experiences and Events

- Grand Prix (Monaco)
- Burning Man festival (USA)
- La Tomatina carnival (Spain)
- Northern Lights

Lodging

- Sail Hotel (Dubai)
- Overwater bungalow
- Five-star hotel or resort
- A penthouse suite

BUCKET

    B – Buy
    U – Undertakings
    C – Create
    K – Kindness
    E – Experiences
    T – Travel

_____

_____

_____

_____

_____

Appendix Two – A Selection of Bucket List Ideas

TRAVEL

T – Transport
R – Restaurants and Food
A – Activities and Adventure
V – Visit
E – Experiences and Events
L – Lodging

APPENDIX THREE – BUCKET LIST 100 ITEMS TEMPLATE

Feel free to use this template during the initial brainstorm of bucket list ideas or for the final draft of your bucket list.

BUCKET LIST

NAME _____

1 _____

2 _____

3 _____

4 _____

5 _____

6 _____

7 _____

Appendix Three – Bucket List 100 Items Template

8 _____

9 _____

10 _____

11 _____

12 _____

13 _____

14 _____

15 _____

16 _____

17 _____

18 _____

19 _____

20 _____

21 _____

22 _____

23 _____

24 _____

25 _____

Appendix Three – Bucket List 100 Items Template

26 _____

27 _____

28 _____

29 _____

30 _____

31 _____

32 _____

33 _____

34 _____

35 _____

36 _____

37 _____

38 _____

39 _____

40 _____

41 _____

42 _____

43 _____

Appendix Three – Bucket List 100 Items Template

44 _____

45 _____

46 _____

47 _____

48 _____

49 _____

50 _____

51 _____

52 _____

53 _____

54 _____

55 _____

56 _____

57 _____

58 _____

59 _____

60 _____

61 _____

Appendix Three – Bucket List 100 Items Template

62 _____

63 _____

64 _____

65 _____

66 _____

67 _____

68 _____

69 _____

70 _____

71 _____

72 _____

73 _____

74 _____

75 _____

76 _____

77 _____

78 _____

79 _____

Appendix Three – Bucket List 100 Items Template

80 _____

81 _____

82 _____

83 _____

84 _____

85 _____

86 _____

87 _____

88 _____

89 _____

90 _____

91 _____

92 _____

93 _____

94 _____

95 _____

96 _____

97 _____

Appendix Three – Bucket List 100 Items Template

98 _____

99 _____

100 _____

WHOOP WHOOP!

READER GIFT: THE HAPPY20

There is no doubt that a bucket list will change your life, but it is also important to remember to squeeze the best out every single day. To remind you of this, I created

THE HAPPY20
20 Free Ways to Boost Happiness in 20 Seconds or Less

A PDF gift for you with quick ideas to improve mood and add a little sparkle to your day.

Head to **JulieSchooler.com/gift** and grab your copy today.

ABOUT THE AUTHOR

Julie had aspirations of being a writer since she was very young but somehow got sidetracked into the corporate world. After the birth of her first child, she rediscovered her creative side. You can find her at JulieSchooler.com.

Her *Easy Peasy* books provide simple and straightforward information on parenting topics. The *Nourish Your Soul* series shares delicious wisdom to feel calmer, happier and more fulfilled.

Busy people can avoid wasting time searching for often confusing and conflicting advice and instead spend time with the beautiful tiny humans in their lives and do what makes their hearts sing.

Julie lives with her family in a small, magnificent country at the bottom of the world where you may find her trying to bake the perfect chocolate brownie.

 facebook.com/JulieSchoolerAuthor
 instagram.com/julie.schooler
twitter.com/JulieSchooler

BOOKS BY JULIE SCHOOLER

Easy Peasy **Books**
Easy Peasy Potty Training
Easy Peasy Healthy Eating

Nourish Your Soul **Books**
Rediscover Your Sparkle
Crappy to Happy
Embrace Your Awesomeness
Bucket List Blueprint
Super Sexy Goal Setting
Find Your Purpose in 15 Minutes
Clutter-Free Forever

Children's Picture Books
Maxy-Moo Flies to the Moon

Collections
Change Your Life 3-in-1 Collection
Rebelliously Happy 3-in-1 Collection

Workbooks
Bucket List Blueprint Workbook
Super Sexy Goal Setting Workbook
Find Your Purpose in 15 Minutes Workbook

JulieSchooler.com/books

ACKNOWLEDGMENTS

This book is the result of some serious 'kick up the proverbial' coaching by two amazing women: Joanna Penn and Louise Thompson. What Joanna doesn't know about indie publishing is not worth knowing. Louise and the Wellbeing Warriors tribe inspire me to improve every day. Thank you and Namaste.

Thanks to all of my friends who helped me with ideas for the Top40 Bucket List, joined me as I checked off items and did not grumble when I couldn't meet up as I was 'doing that wacky bucket list thing again'. Your support and interest in my big, hairy, audacious challenge is the only reason I completed it all.

To Andrew and our two beautiful tiny humans, Dylan and Eloise. I live in a perpetual state of astonishment about how fortunate my life is. Thank you for making me laugh every single day.

PLEASE LEAVE A REVIEW

Bucket List Blueprint

WORKBOOK

Everything You Need to Start a Bucket List That Brings Your Dreams to Life

THANK YOU FOR READING THIS BOOK

I devoted many months to researching and writing this book. I then spent more time having it professionally edited, working with a designer to create an awesome cover and launching it into the world.

Time, money and heart has gone into this book and I very much hope you enjoyed reading it as much as I loved creating it.

It would mean the world to me if you could spend a few minutes writing a review on Goodreads or the online store where you purchased this book.

Please Leave a Review

A review can be as short or long as you like and should be helpful and honest to assist other potential buyers of the book.

Reviews provide social proof that people like and recommend the book. More book reviews mean more book sales which means I can write more books.

Your book review helps me, as an independent author, more than you could ever know. I read every single review and when I get five-star review it absolutely makes my day.

Thanks, Julie.

REFERENCES

Websites and Online Resources

Bucketlist.org

Bucketlistjourney.net

Bucketlist.net

Thebucketlistfamily.com

Daringtolivefully.com

Lifelisted.com

Fullylived.com

Thebucketlistguy.com

Budgetbucketlist.com

Randomactsofkindness.org

The Bucket List Life podcast

Various TEDx talks on bucket lists, goal setting and living more fully

References

Books

59 Seconds – Change Your Life in Under a Minute – Richard Wiseman (USA, 2011)

Authentic Happiness – Using the New Positive Psychology to Realize Your Potential for Lasting Fulfillment – Martin Seligman, Ph.D. (US, 2002)

Feel the Fear and Do It Anyway – How to Turn Your Fear and Indecision into Confidence and Action – Susan Jeffers (UK, 1987)

The Happiness Project – Gretchen Rubin (USA, 2009)

The Secret – Rhonda Byrne (US, 2006)

The Top Five Regrets of the Dying – A Life Transformed by the Dearly Departed – Bronnie Ware (US, 2011)

Thrive – The Third Metric to Redefining Success and Creating a Life of Wellbeing, Wisdom and Wonder – Arianna Huffington (US, 2014)

www.ingramcontent.com/pod-product-compliance
Lightning Source LLC
Chambersburg PA
CBHW072009290426
44109CB00018B/2190